A Young Citizen's Guide to News Literacy

BLURRED LINES
NEWS OR ADVERTISEMENTS?

Cheryl Krajna

PowerKiDS press
New York

Published in 2019 by The Rosen Publishing Group, Inc.
29 East 21st Street, New York, NY 10010

First Edition

Editor: Jill Keppeler
Book Design: Reann Nye

Photo Credits: Cover Steve Debenport/E+/Getty Images; p.4 Everett Historical/Shutterstock.com; p. 5 JGI/Tom Grill/Blend Images/Getty Images; p. 7 Rawpixel.com/Shutterstock.com; p. 9 michaeljung/Shutterstock.com; p. 11 Everett Historical/Shutterstock.com; p. 13 Gary Burchell/DigitalVision/Getty Images; p. 15 Daniel Grill/Getty Images; p. 17 JOSEP LAGO/AFP/Getty Images; p. 19 gchutka/E+/Getty Images; p. 20 Capture Light/Shutterstock.com; p. 21 wavebreakmedia/Shutterstock.com; p. 23 Jeff Greenberg/Universal Images Group/Getty Images; p. 25 StacieStauffSmith Photos/Shutterstock.com; p. 27 (top) Boston Globe/Getty Images; p. 27 (bottom) Bloomberg/Getty Images; p. 29 mirtmirt/Shutterstock.com; p. 30 Dragon Images/Shutterstock.com.

Cataloging-in-Publication Data

Names: Krajna, Cheryl.
Title: Blurred lines: news or advertisements? / Cheryl Krajna.
Description: New York : PowerKids Press, 2019. | Series: A young citizen's guide to news literacy | Includes glossary and index.
Identifiers: ISBN 9781538346068 (pbk.) | ISBN 9781538344972 (library bound) | ISBN 9781538346075 (6 pack)
Subjects: LCSH: Media literacy--Juvenile literature. | Journalism--Juvenile literature. | Mass media--Juvenile literature. | Advertising--Juvenile literature. | Fake news--Juvenile literature.
Classification: LCC P96.M4 K73 2019 | DDC 302.23--dc23

Manufactured in the United States of America

CPSIA Compliance Information: Batch #CWPK19. For Further Information contact Rosen Publishing, New York, New York at 1-800-237-9932

CONTENTS

BEYOND THE HEADLINES, BEHIND THE ADS

"There's a sucker born every minute."

We usually give credit for that saying to P. T. Barnum—showman, museum exhibitor, and circus promoter. Whether he said those words is a matter of **debate**, but what's not debatable is the fact that those words have never been truer.

We live in the time of 24-hour news, with TVs blaring from gas station pumps, on billboards, and in offices and restaurants. Our cell phones beep and ping constantly, alerting us to tweets, likes, and posts. More people than ever before rely on social media sites such as Facebook and Twitter for their news. This constant supply of information may give us only seconds to determine if something we read or hear is true or false, news or advertisement.

BREAKING NEWS

One of P. T. Barnum's earlier jobs was publishing a newspaper, the *Herald of Freedom*, in Danbury, Connecticut. Later, as co-owner of a circus, he used creative promotions to make it the so-called "Greatest Show on Earth."

Sometimes you may feel overwhelmed by all the information you get online and from other sources. In this book, we'll discuss how to sort the good information from the bad and the news from the advertising.

WHAT IS NEWS?

"I've got some news for you!" "Did you hear the news?" We hear these expressions all the time, but what exactly is "news"? To put it simply, news is information. It comes to us from newspapers, TV, radio, websites, podcasts, blogs, and social media. Sometimes news is shared person to person. Sometimes we read it in the school newspaper.

News is something you didn't know before. It's what you read on a news website or hear during a radio broadcast. News is something unusual and important to the world. If we say something is "newsworthy," we mean that it is interesting and valuable, and the average person should know about it. News is **genuine** information. It's based on facts.

BREAKING NEWS

When news reporters gather information for their stories, they use the "Five Ws and an H" to make sure they answer the most important questions: Who? What? Where? When? Why? How?

News comes to us in many different ways, from TV and radio to websites and blogs. It is important to know which news sources are trustworthy and which aren't.

RESEARCH AND REPORT

Sometimes the news is serious, such as when we hear that the government has passed a law. Sometimes the news is happy, such as when we hear that our favorite band will be performing in our town. Sometimes the news can even be funny, such as when we hear about a man who used his lawn mower instead of a snowblower to clean up after a snowstorm.

No matter what the subject is, news is often gathered and shared by reporters. These people typically studied **journalism** in college. Their job is to research, write, and report the news. They go to different events, they meet people, and they learn new things to share with all of us. News can be about anything—politics, crime, sports, even students like you.

BREAKING NEWS

Television stations measure how many people are watching their programs by using ratings. According to Nielsen, a company that counts these viewers, the most-watched news program in America in the 2016-17 season was *60 Minutes*.

Reporters gather information and turn it into news stories or broadcasts.

A BRAVE REPORTER'S ADVENTURES

In 1885, a young woman named Elizabeth Cochrane wrote an angry letter to the editor of a newspaper. The editor was so impressed with her writing that he hired Elizabeth as a reporter! Elizabeth used the **pseudonym** Nellie Bly. In 1889, she set out to beat a fictional record in a new book by Jules Verne—*Around the World in 80 Days.* Nellie Bly beat the book's hero, arriving at her final stop in 72 days!

A BRIEF HISTORY OF NEWS

Humans have always shared news. At first, this took place mostly by word of mouth. In ancient Rome and China, leaders started using written reports to spread information. Much later, during the European Renaissance, business owners shared handwritten newsletters, the roots of the first real newspapers.

America's first newspaper, *Publick Occurrences, Both Foreign and Domestick*, started in 1690, although British leaders quickly stopped its publication. When the *New York Sun* started printing in 1833, it was one of the first newspapers to appeal to regular people.

However, by the early 1960s, polls showed that more Americans got their news from TV than from newspapers. Today, many people get their news from social media—although much of this news is actually from other sources and is just shared on social media sites.

Newsboys gather outside the *Morning Telegraph* office in New York City in 1908, ready to sell the papers on corners across the city. At one time, New York City had dozens of daily and weekly newspapers.

WHAT'S A PRESS CONFERENCE?

When people have news to share, they may host a news conference, inviting reporters to come hear what they have to say. Then reporters share that news with the general public. Back when newspapers were the main source of news, these events were called press conferences, since newspapers were printed on printing presses. Today, they're often called news conferences, since reporters from TV, radio, and other media are there, too.

TRUSTING WHAT YOU SEE

If you've ever read something online (or elsewhere) that you thought was a news story, shared it, then found out the information was wrong, you're not alone. So much information is available today that sometimes it's hard to know what to believe.

Websites for real newspapers, TV stations, and radio stations are good places to start. If a website is full of articles with no authors listed, stay away. For the most part, **random** blogs aren't reliable sources. Generally, random YouTube videos aren't reliable, either.

Another issue is that even usually reliable sources of news must rely on advertising for money. Good news sources don't let advertising and news mix. They don't let advertisers say what the news is, either. However, sometimes these lines get blurred.

BREAKING NEWS

When the University of Missouri Reynolds Journalism Institute asked Americans what news source they trusted most in 2017, the British magazine *The Economist* ranked first! Public television came in second.

If you're unsure if something labeled as a news story is true, become a news detective! Where did the information come from? If it's unclear, you might be reading something that someone made up.

IS IT REAL?

Here are some questions to help you decide if "news" really is news:

- How did you find the story? Was it promoted on a website?
- Is it from a well-known news source, such as a TV station or newspaper website?
- Does it include an author's name?
- Does it include or link to good sources?
- Does the headline use ALL CAPITAL LETTERS for emphasis? Or maybe it uses a lot of exclamation points!!!! That could be the sign of an ad or a fake story.

WHAT IS ADVERTISING?

Businesses often pay for advertisements in media outlets, including newspapers, TV, radio, websites, and social media sites. Ads might be right alongside the news. However, advertising is different from news because it's paid for by a company or person, it's trying to sell you something or promote something, and the buyer controls the complete message.

Sometimes people get confused by news stories and think they're ads, especially if the stories are about a product or upcoming event. And sometimes people think ads are news stories, especially if the advertiser tries to present them as such. There are ways for an educated consumer of the news to be aware of the differences between the two. The best news sources make the lines very clear.

BREAKING NEWS

The Federal Trade Commission (FTC) requires ads to be true, not misleading, and backed up by scientific evidence. These "Truth in Advertising" laws apply to all ads.

If an item—no matter whether it's on a website, in social media, or in a newspaper—is trying to sell you something, it's an ad.

Sometimes, companies or organizations will alert news sources about something they wish to promote. For example, say a **manufacturer** creates a product. News sources don't have to do a story, but they can choose to. Let's say a reporter from a local radio station interviews people at the company, takes notes, and writes a story about the product. It's an overview to give people information. No one tells her exactly what to write. Even though it's about the product, it's a story, not an ad.

However, say that manufacturer pays for a commercial on that radio station. The manufacturer records the message, then the radio station plays it. Because it's paid for, the commercial may include whatever the manufacturer wants and may play multiple times. The commercial is an advertisement.

This news conference is promoting a new smartphone. Reporters at the news conference may write stories telling people about the phone.

WHERE DOES ADVERTISING COME FROM?

Companies spend billions of dollars every year on advertising in the United States. Advertising agencies—businesses that design ads and logos for companies, produce commercials, and purchase the space or time for them to appear—create many of these ads. Advertising agencies help their customers research what consumers want and create messages that people will see, hear, and respond to.

The first question advertisers must answer is: Who is the target audience? Who do they want to see their clients' ads? Then advertisers figure out the best way to reach those people by learning what shows they watch, what websites they visit, how they spend their time on social media, and more. What products target kids like you? Where are you likely to see advertising for those items?

BREAKING NEWS

One of the biggest TV advertising days every year is the day of the Super Bowl. In 2018, 30 seconds of airtime cost more than $5 million—and that didn't include the cost of making the commercial!

Do you ever watch TV and see commercials for toys or foods you want? Think about the ways advertisers try to make products look like something you'd want to buy.

DO YOU REALLY WANT TO EAT THAT?

To make food look as tasty as possible, advertisers may use some weird tricks:

- Glue is used instead of milk in a bowl of cereal so the cereal doesn't get soggy.
- Liquid soap is added to soda to make more bubbles.
- Cardboard is placed between cake layers, then covered with frosting, so the cake doesn't sag.
- Instead of syrup, which makes pancakes soggy, advertisers pour motor oil over stacks of pancakes.

A BRIEF HISTORY OF ADVERTISING

Many years ago, advertising was all by word of mouth. People learned about products and services from each other. After the invention of the printing press, businesses started to use printed advertisements. The first ad appeared in an American newspaper in 1704. In 1742, Benjamin Franklin's *General Magazine* printed the first American magazine ads.

In the 19th century, advertising agencies became a growing business in the United States. By the late 1930s, more money was being spent on radio advertising than magazine ads. The first TV commercial (for a watch) aired in 1941 on over 7,500 TV sets in the New York City area. By the 1990s, however, Internet ads began to change the advertising game again. In 1999, Internet advertising passed $2 billion.

BREAKING NEWS

Company logos are some of the most recognized images in the world. The FedEx logo includes white space between the capital "E" and small "x" in the shape of an arrow—showing that packages are on the move.

The first Internet banner ad ran on the website HotWired.com (the website for *Wired* magazine) in 1994.

GETTING YOUR ATTENTION

Some **techniques** advertisers use include:

- Call to Action: Some ads use orders such as "Act now!"
- Playing on Fears: Ads may claim a product will solve a problem people are worried about, like a health issue.
- Humor: Funny ads get people's attention, and they want to share them with friends and family.
- Repetition: This is when a commercial or ad is used over and over again so you won't forget the product.

KIDS AND ADVERTISING

Advertising isn't aimed just at adults. Kids like you are targeted by advertisers, too! Advertisers connect ads to news about things kids are interested in and entertainment kids like. Maybe a new movie just opened in theaters, and stores are filled with items covered in pictures of the main characters. You can even buy macaroni and cereal that look like them! Movie studios pay a lot of money to make sure you see their characters everywhere.

Also remember that every time you open an app, visit a website, or post to social media, you leave a digital trail. Sometimes companies buy that information. Advertisers pay big bucks to learn what kids like you enjoy, what your friends like, and what you might want to buy from them.

BREAKING NEWS

Tobacco companies targeted kids for many years. However, they're no longer allowed to aim advertising at those under 18. For example, they can't use cartoons to market cigarettes.

Many times, advertisers will tie toys to movies. Do you recognize these characters? The advertisers hope so!

THINK ABOUT IT!

Because news and advertising can be so linked, being a thoughtful consumer of the news means being a thoughtful consumer of advertising, too. Don't be fooled by clever words or a funny picture. Advertisers use all their know-how to get you and your friends to buy what they're selling.

Be smart. Ask yourself: Who is responsible for the ad? Look for a company name or logo. What does the ad want you to do? When looking at a website, think about who created the site. Is the site meant to teach you something or to sell you something? Does an ad make an object or experience look better than it is? How is a photo in an ad different from a photo in a news story?

BREAKING NEWS

Some famous creators once worked in advertising. Theodor Geisel, better known as Dr. Seuss, wrote and illustrated ads for General Electric and other companies. Muppets creator Jim Henson made more than 100 commercials for a coffee company.

Companies sometimes pay to name sports arenas and fields after their business. This football field in Pittsburgh, Pennsylvania, is named after the H. J. Heinz Company, which makes foods such as ketchup.

DON'T LET ADVERTISERS TRICK YOU

- If something gets your attention, think about how and why. What words, images, or sounds did the advertiser use?
- How did you feel before seeing a particular ad, and how do you feel after? Ads want you to buy something, so you may now want something you didn't even know about a minute ago!
- Always get a parent's permission before you click on an ad or fill out any form online.

CHANGING TIMES

In some ways, it used to be easier to tell ads from news and entertainment. For one thing, there were fewer places you might see ads. They'd be on newspaper pages, but it'd be easy to recognize them. With online news sources and social media, things can be different—and older media sources are changing, too.

Social media sites have ads, but can you tell one when you see one? Businesses can pay to have links and posts promoted above others. Just because they're promoted doesn't mean they're good or trustworthy! Look for small labels that say "**sponsored**" or "promoted." Your favorite sports star could tweet about a certain brand of sneakers. Was he paid to do this? If so, that's an ad, even if it's not labeled!

BREAKING NEWS

The Society of Professional Journalists (SPJ) has a code of **ethics** for those working in the news business. Principles in this code include making sure news and advertisements are clearly labeled and not giving favored treatment to advertisers.

...ry weather Eagles' storm?

...one. The ...tack pre-...em. If the ...they can ...there is ...Faibanks ...pass de-...getting

...e biggest ...vers we'll ...gainst all ...ko, (Har-... is proba-... in the ...Charles ...nd (Don) ...3. ...hat we're ...have to ...well. We ...guys on

alone back there with that kind of height. All there quarterbacks would have to do in that situation is throw the ball up in the air and let them jump over us to get it.

"We have to put a lot of people around the football. Our linebackers are going to have to take good drops. Our defensive line has to put some pressure on the quarterback.

"In our first game (vs. Giants) we weren't that well coordinated. Last Sunday against Minnesota we got better, and in this one we'll have to improve over that."

Roman Gabriel and young Mike Boryla will be throwing for the Eagles. Gabriel is staging a comeback after an off-season in '74, when Borlya, as a rookie, took over the first-string job and directed the Eagles to three late-season victories.

Gabriel, however, felt he was too light (205 pounds) a year ago, and has put on 25 pounds to become stronger.

"We have two cans of their films to look at this week," said Durko. "Gabriel was a little erratic in the first game, but he did throw well last week against Cleveland."

But Bóryla is pushing him hard for the top job, which only spells trouble for the Pats. Either way — Gabriel or Boryla — their pass defense is going to be under pressure.

...roster

...eteran's Stadium, 8 p.m.

POS	HGT	WGT	AGE	NFL EXP	COLLEGE
K	6-0	185	26	2	Southhampton (Eng)
P	6-0	213	22	R	Mississippi State
QB	6-4	200	22	R	Kansas State
QB	6-3	200	25	2	Wisconsin
QB	6-2	212	27	5	Stanford
WR	5-10	170	26	5	Stanford
RB	5-11	208	22	R	Southern Cal
S	6-1	186	26	5	Southern Cal
RB	5-10	210	24	2	Holy Cross

PATRIOTS NOTEBOOK

Cunningham doubtful against Eagles tonight

AMHERST — Sam Cunningham (hip pointer), Bob Geddes (fractured hand) and Andy Johnson (dislocated toe) are all doubtful for tonight's game in Philadelphia. The three were injured last Sunday against

Texas Tech ... The Patriots also waived linebacker Gail Clark.

THINK FALL
THINK FOOTBALL!

You'll enjoy summer more

It's easy to tell where the ad is on this newspaper page from 1975, but can you tell when stories are sponsored on a modern website or app?

LOOK CAREFULLY

As older forms of news media lose readers, listeners, and viewers, some of those media sources are turning to advertising tricks from other places. "Native advertising" means ads that don't look like ads. They might look like news stories or blog posts. These types of stories or posts are supposed to be clearly labeled, but you might have to look carefully for the label.

An advertorial also looks like a regular news article, so you might not realize it's an ad. The word combines the words "advertising" and "editorial." When you click on an online advertorial, it takes you to the advertiser's website. Sometimes entire publications, print or online, might be composed of advertorials. If you see lots of brand names, it's probably an advertorial, not news!

When you search for a subject online, pay attention to the search results. The first few are likely to be websites that paid to be first on the list! They're not always—or even mostly—the best sources.

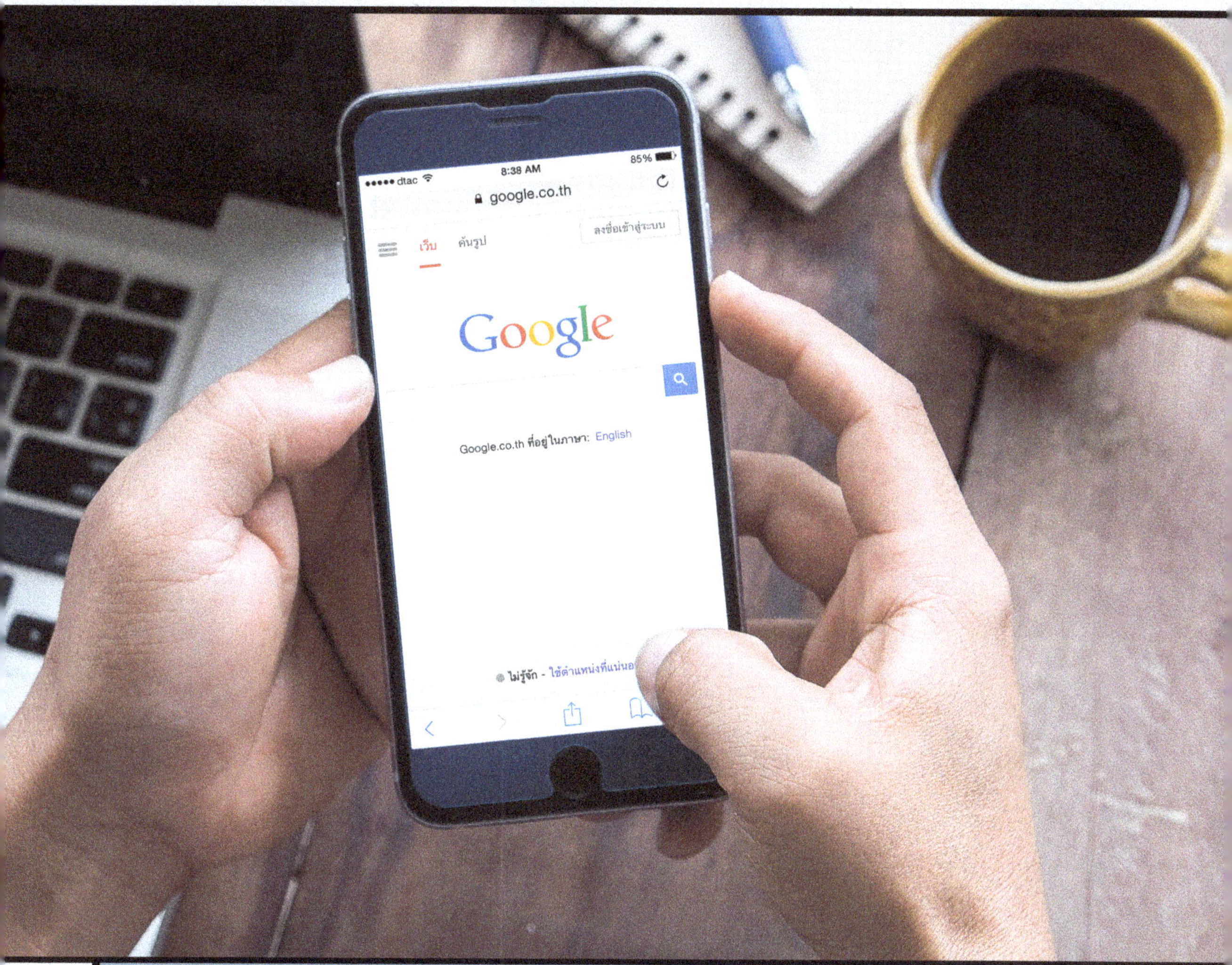

CLUES TO LOOK FOR

How can you tell native advertising or advertorials from news content? Here are some things to look for:

- Do you see "sponsored" or "promoted"? What about "paid content"?
- Who wrote it? Was it the representative of a business connected to the **text**? If so, it's probably an ad of some sort.
- Does it appear in an established news outlet? Do you recognize the name? These sources are more likely to be **legitimate**—or at least clearly labeled.

CHECK THE FACTS!

The average young person sees more than 3,000 ads a day on TV, online, on billboards, and in magazines. "Fake news"—which can include ads posing as stories—spreads faster than ever, thanks to how much people rely on social media, where it's very easy to share articles and spread bad sources.

Don't be fooled. Ask questions about what you read and hear. If something you read or see online interests you, learn more to make sure it's legitimate. Use different sources, such as books and magazines. Ask yourself how you found the information. Was it promoted on a website? Did it appear on social media? Does the article say who wrote it? Be your own editor. Check the facts. And don't believe everything you read!

It's important to pay attention to sources. Be a wise consumer of the news—and ads!

GLOSSARY

debate: An argument or public discussion.

ethics: Rules based on what's right and what's wrong.

genuine: True or real.

journalism: The collecting, writing, and editing of news stories for newspapers, magazines, websites, television, or radio.

legitimate: Real or accepted.

manufacturer: A company or person who makes a product.

pseudonym: A name used instead of a real name.

random: Something without a pattern or plan, or something chosen without a pattern or plan.

sponsor: To pay for or plan and carry out a project or activity.

technique: A method of accomplishing a task.

text: The words that make up a book, website, or another piece of writing.

INDEX

WEBSITES

Due to the changing nature of Internet links, PowerKids Press has developed an online list of websites related to the subject of this book. This site is updated regularly. Please use this link to access the list: www.powerkidslinks.com/newslit/blurred